Moments Together

for

A PEACEFUL HOME

DENNIS and BARBARA RAINEY

Regal

From Gospel Light
Ventura, California, U.S.A.

Regal

PUBLISHED BY REGAL BOOKS
FROM GOSPEL LIGHT
VENTURA, CALIFORNIA, U.S.A.
PRINTED IN THE U.S.A.

Regal Books is a ministry of Gospel Light, an evangelical Christian publisher dedicated to serving the local church. We believe God's vision for Gospel Light is to provide church leaders with biblical, user-friendly materials that will help them evangelize, disciple and minister to children, youth and families.

It is our prayer that this Regal book will help you discover biblical truth for your own life and help you meet the needs of others. May God richly bless you.

For a free catalog of resources from Regal Books/Gospel Light, please call your Christian supplier or contact us at 1-800-4-GOSPEL *or* www.regalbooks.com.

Rights for publishing this book in other languages are contracted by Gospel Light Worldwide, the international non-profit ministry of Gospel Light. Gospel Light Worldwide also provides publishing and technical assistance to international publishers dedicated to producing Sunday School and Vacation Bible School curricula and books in the languages of the world. For additional information, visit www.gospellightworldwide.org; write to Gospel Light Worldwide, P.O. Box 3875, Ventura, CA 93006; or send an e-mail to info@gospellightworldwide.org.

The publisher regrets the omission of credits and requests documentation for future printings.

Cover and interior design by Robert Williams
Edited by Stephanie Parrish and Dave Boehi

Library of Congress Cataloging-in-Publication Data
Rainey, Dennis, 1948–
  Moments together for a peaceful home / Dennis and Barbara Rainey.
    p. cm.
  ISBN 0-8307-3251-9
  1. Family—Prayer-books and devotions—English.   I. Rainey, Barbara.
II. Title.
  BV255.R18 2003
  249—dc21   2003009713

1   2   3   4   5   6   7   8   9   /   09   08   07   06   05   04   03

INTRODUCTION

We live in a world of speed and noise, of frayed nerves and hurried schedules, of crushing responsibilities and unrealistic expectations. And sometimes all you want are a few moments of peace.

For some people, peace means a Sunday afternoon nap; for others, it may mean a walk in the forest or an afternoon by a bubbling stream. For married couples, it is those times of contentment and bliss when you can revel in each other's company and enjoy a glimpse of the harmony God can bring to a relationship. For many parents, peace may be a rare commodity that occurs for about five minutes a day—every other week on Saturdays.

We invite you and your spouse to carve out a few minutes each day for some time of peace and rest. Take a break from your schedule and spend some time together reading Scripture and pondering just what you can do to experience more peace in your home on a regular basis.

Moments Together for a Peaceful Home contains 30 brief devotionals for a husband and wife to work through together. Some of the topics we cover:

- Sorting out your priorities
- Making a choice to do something of value with your family
- Finding value in laughter
- Confronting each other—gently
- Forgiving others as God forgives you
- Pleasing your mate
- Dealing with personality differences

The greatest thing you and your spouse can do for your family is to spend a few peaceful moments together learning how you can bring God into your lives and those of your family. Each of these devotionals takes 10 to 15 minutes to complete. We're confident that you'll look forward to these few minutes as the highlight of your day.

Dennis and Barbara Rainey

ANSWERING JESUS' PRAYER

*I do not ask in behalf of these alone, but for those
also who believe in Me through their word;
that they may all be one.*

JOHN 17:20-21

As I reflect on the teachings of Christ, I find that much of His instruction dealt with maintaining peace and harmony in relationships. He taught His disciples to break down barriers in relationships. He taught them to forgive each other. Love was the banner of His earthly ministry.

The Scripture passage above is part of the Savior's high-priestly prayer, prayed near the end of His life. Why did He focus on unity and oneness at this crucial point? Could it be that it was because the strongest demonstration of the Holy Spirit's power in our lives is imperfect Christians living with one another?

But it isn't always easy, is it? When you and your mate—or you and your children—have a conflict with each other, you probably tend to withdraw from intimacy. Then you begin to believe the worst about the other person, and eventually you lash out in anger or bitterly withdraw, allowing the anger to fester.

Communication is vital to maintaining unity. You may have to reinvent your own pony express to stay close, even if it has to run through hostile territory. Maybe you'll have one meal a day when your family sits down and eats together, with the phone off the hook and the television off. Possibly you'll pray with your mate and with each of your children at the end of the day. Or maybe you'll take a walk and talk with a troubled teen who just needs you to be there.

The main thing is to take responsibility for doing your part to see that Jesus' prayer—that you may "be one"—doesn't go unanswered in your family.

Discuss: In your family, how does disharmony typically start? Does fostering family harmony always mean settling kids' differences for them?

Pray: Pray that Christ's prayer for unity will be realized among your family members by their coming together in love, acceptance and forgiveness.

TAKE RESPONSIBILITY
FOR DOING YOUR PART
TO SEE THAT JESUS'
PRAYER—THAT YOU
MAY "BE ONE"—DOESN'T
GO UNANSWERED.

OF FIRST IMPORTANCE

*For what I received I passed on to you as of
first importance: that Christ died for our sins according
to the Scriptures, that he was buried, that he was raised
on the third day according to the Scriptures.*

1 CORINTHIANS 15:3-4 (*NIV*)

The Bible is a collection of many books and has many truths to teach us. We are blessed that in this passage the apostle Paul singles out its core truth. Of course nothing in Scripture is unimportant, but nothing else is "of first importance" like the death, burial and resurrection of Jesus.

What do all of us—children, teens and adults—need to know to make the significance of Jesus's death, burial and resurrection real in our lives? First, *we need to know who God is and how He loves us.* We need to know what sets Him apart from humans:

- God is holy; He is perfect. People, however, are not perfect.
- God is just; He is always fair. We are not just in all our decisions.
- God is love; He desires a relationship with us—

that's why He sent His Son. We are not always motivated out of our love for another.

Second, *we need to know that our sins must be forgiven* (see Rom. 6:23). Many people in this culture of tolerance feel uncomfortable talking about hell. God is patient, but He is not tolerant. His justice calls for an atonement (a payment, a penalty) for people's sins. We must understand that our sins can keep us out of heaven. Our sins must be paid for. And that is what Jesus Christ did for us on the cross.

Finally, *we need to know that we receive God's forgiveness through faith in Jesus Christ* (see Eph. 2:8-9). Faith involves repenting of our sins, turning to God in faith and trusting Jesus Christ to be our Savior and Lord. When we repent, we acknowledge our sins before God and express our sorrow for our sins to Him.

These are the basics that we all need to know about that which is "of first importance."

Discuss: Have you made these truths about Jesus' death, burial and resurrection "of first importance" in your lives? Have you explained these truths to your children?

Pray: If you have not yet received God's forgiveness through faith in Jesus Christ, consider doing so now.

Here's a sample prayer: "Lord Jesus, I need You. Thank You for dying on the cross for my sins. I open the door of my life and receive You as my Savior and Lord. Thank You for forgiving my sins and giving me eternal life. Make me the kind of person You want me to be." Also pray that God would work in your children's hearts to bring them to Him.

NOTHING ELSE IS "OF FIRST
IMPORTANCE" LIKE THE
DEATH, BURIAL AND
RESURRECTION
OF JESUS.

OF SECOND IMPORTANCE

Lay up for yourselves treasures in heaven,
where neither moth nor rust destroys, and where
thieves do not break in or steal; for where your
treasure is, there will your heart be also.

MATTHEW 6:20-21

You and your mate would benefit from spending some time singling out what is of second importance to you. Barbara and I have pondered and struggled with this issue for years. Among the core values we have listed are compassion, discipline, courage, integrity and the fear of the Lord.

One day as we were prayerfully interacting over our individual core values, we made a profound discovery: Our priorities were different! One of Barbara's top five values was "teaching our children the work ethic." I didn't even list that in my top ten! Nor did she have one of my top five core values down on her sheet—"relationships."

Suddenly it became clear why our weekend schedule sometimes felt like a battlefield. We were battling over values—work versus relationships. Barbara wanted to use our

Saturdays to work on the house or in the yard. My preference was to slip away (from the work) and go build memories and relationships on a boat on the lake.

Neither value was wrong—just different.

That day we learned a lesson I will never forget: Each of us spends our time on those things we feel are most important. And because most of us never get around to defining our core values as individuals and as a family, we end up living scattered and hectic lives, driven by unreal expectations.

Discuss: Write a mission statement for your family, listing the core values you would like to emphasize. Do the ways you spend most of your time and money reflect these values?

Pray: Pray that God will help you choose the most important values for your family and help you spend your time and finances in ways that honor Him.

DO SOMETHING OF VALUE TONIGHT
(PART ONE)

Therefore be careful how you walk, not as unwise men,
but as wise, making the most of your time.

EPHESIANS 5:15-16

*D*riving home one night after work a number of years ago, I switched on the radio to catch the news. In a moment of uncharacteristic sincerity, the announcer made a statement that sliced through my fog of fatigue: "I hope you did something of value today. You wasted a whole day if you didn't."

His statement struck me abruptly. Fortunately, I felt pretty good about how I had invested my time that day, solving some of the problems of a swiftly growing organization. But in 10 minutes I would be home, where one lovely lady and six pairs of little eyes would need my attention.

Would I do something of value with them tonight?

It's just one night, I thought, *and besides, I'm exhausted.* Then I pondered how one night followed by another, 365 times, adds up to a year. The nights and years seemed to be passing with increasing velocity.

Five more minutes and I'd be home.

I'll bet there are other men like me who are really tired right now. I'll bet I do better than average with my kids, I smugly concluded.

But another question came to mind and lingered: *Did God call me to be merely a better-than-average husband and father? Or to be obedient and to excel?*

But it's just one night. What would I accomplish? Would I waste it spending all evening in front of the television? Or invest it in planting the seeds of a positive legacy?

I wanted just one evening of selfishness—to do my own thing. But what if Barbara had a similar attitude? Then who would carry the baton?

One more minute and I'd be home.

Just one night, Lord. It's just one night. But then the same angel who wrestled Jacob to the ground pinned me with a half nelson as I drove into the garage.

Okay, Lord, You've got me.

Discuss: Did you do something of value today? If you didn't, you just wasted a whole day of your life.

Pray: Ask God to help you keep your priorities straight amid the pressures you face and the demanding schedule you keep. Ask Him to give you courage to do what's right.

DID GOD CALL ME TO
BE MERELY A BETTER-THAN-
AVERAGE HUSBAND AND
FATHER? OR TO BE OBEDIENT
AND TO EXCEL?

DO SOMETHING OF VALUE TONIGHT
(PART TWO)

*So then do not be foolish, but understand
what the will of the Lord is.*

EPHESIANS 5:17

$\mathcal{A}$s the kids surrounded my car like a band of whooping Indians, screaming "Daddy! Daddy! Daddy!" I was glad on this night I had made the right choice.

At supper, rather than just grazing our way through the meal, we spent a few moments on nostalgia. Each of us answered the question, What was your favorite thing we did as a family this past year?

After supper I gave the kids three choices of what we could do: play Monopoly together, read a good book together or wrestle together on the living-room floor. Which do you think they chose?

Three little sumo wrestlers grabbed my legs as they began to drag me into the living room. Dad was pinned by the kids. Mom was tickled by Dad. And kids went flying through the air (literally) for the next hour. Even our ten-month-old got into the act by pouncing on me after she had observed the other kids in action.

Will the kids remember? Maybe, but I doubt it.

Did I waste the evening? No. With the power that God supplies, I did my best to leave a legacy that counts—a legacy of love that will outlive me. I was reminded of two things. First, I thought of Paul's words in Ephesians 5:17, in which he reminded us to make the most of our time and to "not be foolish."

Second, I remembered my dad. He was badgered by one determined boy into playing catch over and over again. I can still remember his well-worn mitt and curve ball.

If you struggle with priorities as I do, you might want to commit to memory this verse in Ephesians. The fool whom Paul wrote about is someone we never intend to become; it just happens—one day at a time.

I hope you did something of value today. And I hope you will tonight as well.

Discuss: What choices do you often have to make to balance your own needs with those of your family? Do you ever resent these demands? What is one goal for family time that you want to achieve in the coming year?

Pray: Ask God to give you favor as you invest your lives in one another and in your children.

FATHERS AS SERVANT-LEADERS

For the husband is the head of the wife, as Christ also is the head of the church. Husbands, love your wives, just as Christ also loved the church and gave Himself up for her.

EPHESIANS 5:23,25

Our culture has spent more than two decades redefining the roles of husband and wife. At one extreme is the Oklahoma newspaper headline that read, "State House Repeals Law Appointing Husbands as Head of Household." At the other extreme is the man who thinks being the head of the house means his wife must obey his every whim without question.

But the Scriptures clearly give us the model for being not only a man but also a husband and father. I call that model the servant-leader. According to this model, husbands and fathers are *to lead, to love* and *to serve.*

Merriam Webster's Collegiate Dictionary defines a leader as a "guide," or "conductor," "a person who has commanding authority or influence"—a person who shows the way, directs and governs. God designed these roles of husband and father, and the mantle of leadership comes along with them.

Flowing out of the responsibility to lead is the responsibility for husbands to *love their wives*—unconditionally. I can't help but wonder what must go through kids' minds today as moms and dads have verbal slugfests. As leaders of the family, dads need—more than ever—to affirm their commitments to their wives and children.

Serving his wife rounds out the role of a husband and father. Some men cannot understand the biblical definition of a leader as "a servant." Even though He was Lord, Jesus said that "the Son of Man did not come to be served, but to serve" (Matt. 20:28).

As your wife's servant, can you name her top three needs? What worries her? What circumstances quickly put her emotional gas tank on empty?

Men, let me challenge you *to lead*, *to love* and *to serve*.

Discuss: As a father, rate yourself from one (highest) to five in each of the three categories: leading, loving and serving. See if you can answer the questions in this devotional's next-to-the-last paragraph.

Pray: Men, pray that you will have the sensitivity to love and the humility to serve and lead your wives.

AS LEADERS OF THE FAMILY,
DADS NEED—MORE THAN
EVER—TO AFFIRM THEIR
COMMITMENTS TO THEIR
WIVES AND CHILDREN.

THE PROVERBS 31 WOMAN?

An excellent wife, who can find? For her worth is far above jewels.

PROVERBS 31:10

One of our favorite types of broadcasts on *FamilyLife Today* has been the mom-check day. We would call some stay-at-home mothers we knew from around the country and ask how their day was going.

I always enjoyed asking these women how their houses looked. A woman in Dallas with a new baby said, "Our bedroom's a disaster! Nicole's cradle is in there. The swing's in there. My desk has become a makeshift changing table. Diapers are all over. We've gotten 30 million gifts of girls' outfits, and the corners are filled with clothes."

We called my wife, Barbara, and she described the kitchen: "Oh, it's a mess, as always. Let's see. We still have blueberry muffins out. There are dishes in the sink and crumbs on the floor, and laundry that I folded this morning is on the dining-room table. And a basket that's mounded with ready-to-be-folded laundry is sitting on a chair."

Then there was Brenda, a friend in Portland. I loved her comment: "Our house is a wreck. The kitchen is filled with dirty dishes. But it's been a great day. My priorities have been in order."

I know that many people look upon the wife and mother described in Proverbs 31 as some sort of superwoman, who ran the perfect household. But let me ask you this: Do you think her home was dirty at times? Do you think she always folded her laundry?

While this woman was praised—"She looks well to the ways of her household, and does not eat the bread of idleness" (v. 27)—she was not perfect. The way I see it, her praise was based not on the neatness of her household but on the priorities by which she lived.

One of the great tragedies of recent decades is that too many people judge the performance of a housewife by the tidiness of her home. We need to be able to pull back and know what's important. You may have a floor that needs to be mopped or a refrigerator that needs to be cleaned. You may have kids with sniffles. It all feels like it's pressing in on you. But 10 to 15 years from now, what is going to matter? What will your kids recall most about you?

Do you want to be remembered for the love you gave your children and the godly character you modeled for them?

Discuss: How important is keeping a clean house to you? Why?

Pray: Ask God to help you keep your perspective as you fulfill your responsibilities as wife and mother. Men, pray for your wives—then help them!

LOOSE LIPS
SINK SHIPS

Let no unwholesome word proceed from your mouth,
but only such a word as is good for edification.

EPHESIANS 4:29

I often think of the World War II slogan that was posted as a warning in factories that manufactured ships, ammunitions and supplies: Loose Lips Sink Ships. With the battle for the family being what it is today, perhaps we need to post a similar warning on our refrigerators: Loose Lips Sink Partnerships.

"Unwholesome" literally means "rotten." When something is rotten, there's no mistaking it, is there? Similarly, when a rotten word is spoken, it stinks up the place. Instantly. The foulest-smelling words are negative ones, fueled with anger and aimed at another person.

Paul says that instead of smelling up the place with unwholesome talk, we should say only that which is helpful and uplifting, according to the needs of those who listen. For example, my wife, Barbara, would often feel emotionally empty after orchestrating trips to the dentist, doctor, lessons and meetings, in addition to dealing with all the draining conflicts that would take place in a family of eight. She didn't need me to criticize her for what she hadn't done. She needed me to be on her team, cheering her on and expressing appreciation for all that she did for the kids, the ministry and me.

Occasionally we'd use the dinner table to have a praise-Mom party. Each of us would take turns expressing appreciation and encouragement all around the table. Our teenaged boys would brag, "I like Mom because she cooks good food and a lot of it!" Our youngest would chirp, "I like Mom because she's pretty." Another would say, "I like Mom because she helps me with my homework." Without exception, when we'd finished our praise party, Barbara's countenance had brightened and her shoulders had straightened!

How about having some words with a positive aroma at your house tonight? Pick a family member to build up, and then share what you most appreciate about him or her.

Discuss: Think of areas in which a family member needs a word of encouragement and make specific plans to provide it—a letter, note, call, praise party, etc.

Pray: Ask God to give you sensitivity to know how to use words of edification to build up your spouse and the other members of your family.

LOOSE LIPS SINK PARTNERSHIPS.

PARENTS AS PROTECTORS

Lead me to the rock that is higher than I. For Thou hast been a refuge for me, a tower of strength against the enemy.

PSALM 61:2-3

Although God, as the psalmist said, is our ultimate Security and Protector, parents also are to serve as "a tower of strength" for their children. Some of my most vivid childhood memories are of the hours we spent in our family's storm cellar while severe thunderstorms rumbled overhead. As I reflect back on the numerous visits to that musty cellar, I can't help but ponder the need for parents to protect their children during the storms that rumble through their lives.

It might be helpful for me to clarify what I mean by "protecting children." First, I do not mean shielding them from making decisions on their own or so controlling their lives that they do not grow up emotionally, mentally and spiritually. I do not mean smothering children with overprotection or insulating them from making mistakes or taking risks.

What I do mean by "protecting children" is *being proactively involved in their lives to prepare them for crucial decisions, problems and pressures.* For example, you protect them when

- you tell them what to do if a stranger offers a ride or candy to them;
- you offer advice on how to handle a bully in their neighborhood or school;
- you help them develop good friendships and step in when a negative influence seems to be getting the upper hand;
- you give them boundaries—like placing a limit on the types of movies they see;
- you love them enough to talk about a difficult issue like sex or to set rules for dating (when they can begin, what types of dates they can start out with, etc.);
- you pray for God's protection over them when you cannot be with them (see Matt. 18:10).

Are you providing a strong tower of protection for your children?

Discuss: A tower provides an excellent view of approaching enemies. What enemies, or issues, are your children facing now? What enemies do you see on the horizon? How can you prepare your children to face these enemies?

Pray: Ask God for the wisdom and courage to be able to protect your children.

PARENTS NEED TO
PROTECT THEIR CHILDREN
DURING THE STORMS
THAT RUMBLE THROUGH
THEIR LIVES.

WHO IS YOUR ENEMY?

For our struggle is not against flesh and blood.

EPHESIANS 6:12

A lot of jokes picture marriage as a battlefield. One anonymous author wrote, "Marriage is the only war where you sleep with the enemy."

I would rather picture the entire world as the true battlefield and your marriage as God's smallest battle formation for winning the war. In truth, your marriage is taking place on a spiritual battlefield, not a romantic balcony.

Every married couple needs to understand the following biblical principle: Your mate is not your enemy.

Picture your marriage as two people joined together in a foxhole, cooperating in battle against a common enemy. Take a good look at your own foxhole. Are you fighting the enemy or each other? As a friend of ours told me, "I was so busy standing up in the foxhole, duking it out with my husband, that I had no time to be involved in fighting against the real enemy."

Keep in mind that whenever you declare war on your mate, ultimately you are opposing God Himself. You are rejecting the person He provided to complete you, to meet your needs.

Here's a practical test to discover if you view your mate as an enemy or as a fellow soldier. Do you focus on the negative in your mate or on the positive? When you marry, you're so caught up in your new spouse that he or she can seem to do no wrong. But within 12,000 miles or 12 months, whichever comes first, you reverse the process. You are now so focused on what your mate does wrong that you are oblivious to what he or she does right!

I love Robert Lewis Stevenson's exhortation to us as we look at our spouses. He says, "Make the most of the best and the least of the worst."

Discuss: Who is your real enemy? Think back to times when you have forgotten who your real enemy is—how did that impact your marriage and family? Do you treat your mate as a partner or as an enemy?

Pray: Pray that God would make you aware of the true battle and enemy you face each day and of how you need each other on that battlefield.

DO YOU VIEW YOUR
MATE AS AN ENEMY
OR AS A FELLOW SOLDIER
AGAINST A
COMMON ENEMY?

DAY 11

THE GREATEST GIFT

Let marriage be held in honor among all.

HEBREWS 13:4

I will never forget the quarrel between my parents when I was in first grade. I was sitting in my pajamas, listening to them argue—I can't even remember what it was about. I do remember thinking, *Are Mom and Dad going to get a divorce?* Now, this was back in the early 1950s, when divorce was rare; it was hardly even talked about back then.

If I had that fear at that age, what must the average first grader today feel? Kids today are surrounded by divorce.

The greatest gift you can give your children is a sacred commitment to your spouse. You must keep your marriage relationship a priority. Your kids need your devotion to each other more than they need your devotion to them.

A woman once wrote me about the changes she experienced in her relationship with her ex-husband after attending a FamilyLife Marriage Conference. They had been divorced three years when they went. She wrote,

> I really did not want to go. As far as I was concerned, our relationship was dead. The conference changed

our lives. As we listened to what the Bible said about marriage, the roles of husband and wife, we realized we had done it all wrong. As a result of the conference, we decided to start dating again. Four months later, we were remarried.

She concluded,

Our remarriage is a dream come true for our six-year-old son. He can hardly believe that the thing he wanted most has really happened. His mommy and daddy are together again.

Few things can harden the heart of a child more than the divorce of his or her parents. Your kids need a mom and a dad who are committed to each other.

Discuss: How much time do you spend with your mate on a daily and weekly basis? When was the last time you did something to cultivate your relationship?

Pray: Ask God to preserve your legacy by protecting your marriage. Ask Him for His favor on your marriage.

"WASTING TIME" TOGETHER

For I am mindful of the sincere faith within you,
which first dwelt in your grandmother Lois, and your mother
Eunice, and I am sure that it is in you as well.

2 TIMOTHY 1:5

The *Encyclopaedia Britannica* devotes a half page to the accomplishments of Charles Francis Adams, the son of President John Quincy Adams. The younger Adams followed the political trail of his father and became a United States diplomat to Great Britain. The encyclopedia makes no mention of Charles's family, but Charles's diary does. One day's entry read: "Went fishing with my son today—a day wasted."

Another diary, however, offers a different perspective on the same event: "Went fishing with my father—the most wonderful day of my life!" The person who wrote those words was Charles's son Brook.

Interesting, isn't it, how a little boy's perspective can be so different from his dad's?

But it's true of me, too. I can remember a fishing trip with Dad to Canada, where I caught a trophy northern pike. And I remember another outing to a local lake where he netted my tiny catfish—a fish so small that it escaped through the holes in the net. He always kidded me about that fish. His laughter still echoes in my mind.

It's interesting how my adult mind can play tricks on me. Looking back, those days of vacation memories are among my most cherished possessions. Yet as an adult, I've sometimes found myself thinking that I don't have time for playing catch and going fishing with my own kids—until I reflect on the value God places on a little boy or little girl.

Discuss: Do you have special memories from your childhood of an adult taking time just to be with you? What spiritual values did you learn? Do you as a parent try to spend some time alone with each of your children every week?

Pray: Pray that God will give you wisdom to see what is really important in your schedule. Ask Him to give you the courage to say no to the less important so that you can say yes to spending quality time with your children.

I sometimes find myself thinking that I don't have time for playing catch and going fishing with my kids—until I reflect on the value God places on a little boy or little girl.

THE GENTLE ART OF CONFRONTATION

But speaking the truth in love, we are to grow up in all aspects into Him, who is the head, even Christ.

EPHESIANS 4:15

No family is without conflicts; and when we let conflicts simmer without confrontation, they have a habit of boiling over and affecting our spiritual lives.

William Wordsworth said, "He who has a good friend needs no mirror." Family members can learn to be each other's best friend by learning the gentle art of confrontation. Blessed is the marriage in which both spouses feel the other is a good friend—one who will listen and then respond, who will understand and who will work through whatever needs to be dealt with. Occasionally this requires loving confrontation.

Of course, we must face the fact that some of us don't want to be confronted. Some people would rather be comfortable than Christlike. Many of Barbara's most valuable insights to me are the ones that hurt a bit, but I need to hear them because they keep me on the right track.

Loving confrontation starts with love. As 1 Corinthians 13 points out, love expects the best of others. There's no way to confront someone else productively if you expect the worst or have a chip on your shoulder.

Loving confrontation is not nagging. It states its position without dragging it out for days. Being nagged is no fun. Someone has said it's like being nibbled to death by a duck.

Christian confrontation doesn't accuse; it focuses on "I" language, with my saying plainly how I feel. It avoids "you" language, which inevitably sounds condemning. There's a world of difference between saying "I really don't like arriving at church late—can I do something to help?" and "You always make us late!"

Also keep in mind that the people you love but need to confront are not your enemies. Your mate is never your enemy. Christian confrontation requires that you speak the truth—but always in love.

Discuss: Are there areas of agitation that you try to ignore in order to keep a smooth relationship? Are you being honest with yourself and with those you love? When should you bring up a problem issue?

Pray: Pray for the courage to confront—lovingly—and also for the wisdom to know how to speak the truth in love.

CHRISTIAN
CONFRONTATION
REQUIRES THAT YOU
SPEAK THE TRUTH—BUT
ALWAYS IN LOVE.

WHO ARE YOU TO JUDGE?

Do not judge lest you be judged. For in the way you judge, you will be judged; and by your standard of measure, it will be measured to you.

MATTHEW 7:1-2

Perhaps the greatest roadblock to loving confrontation is the well-known log that seems lodged in your eyes (see Matt. 7:3-5). Such handicapped vision inevitably distorts our relationships, both with God and with each other.

Here are five tips Barbara and I have found useful in keeping judgment out of confrontation:

1. *Check your motivation.* Are you bringing this up to help or to hurt? Prayer is the best way to check your motives. When you take the situation to God and He shines His light on you and the problem, then you usually see your motivation for what it is.

2. *Check your attitude.* Loving confrontation says "I care about you." Don't hop on your bulldozer and bury your mate.

3. *Check the circumstance.* Pick a suitable time, location and setting. Don't confront your mate the moment he or she walks in the door after a hard day's work, at mealtime or in front of others.
4. *Check to see what other pressures may be present.* Be sensitive to where others are coming from. What's going on in their lives right now?
5. *Be ready to take it as well as dish it out.* Sometimes, confronting someone can boomerang—he or she may have some stuff saved up for you that will spill out when you bring up an issue. If you expect others to listen, to understand, to hear you out and to accept your point of view, be ready to do the same yourself.

Discuss: Think of an issue or complaint you may want to air with your mate. Ask yourself if you are projecting—seeing your own faults in your mate. Before confronting your mate, reflect on whether the issue might be solved by "weeding your own garden" first.

Pray: Pray that you can see your marriage relationship objectively and that you are willing to be judged by the same standards you hold for your mate.

LOVING CONFRONTATION SAYS
"I CARE ABOUT YOU."

GOD'S LANDMARKS

*Bless the LORD, O my soul, and forget none of
His benefits; who pardons all your iniquities; who heals
all your diseases; who redeems your life from the pit; who
crowns you with lovingkindness and compassion;
who satisfies your years with good things, so that
your youth is renewed like the eagle.*

PSALM 103:2-5

God provides landmarks in the Scriptures so that we will "forget none of His benefits." Perhaps one of the oldest landmarks that God gave us is the rainbow.

After Noah survived the flood, God said that the rainbow would remind people of His judgment and mercy. He had judged the earth by water and destroyed it, but He never would destroy it again by water. A rainbow, set in the sky for us to observe, is a constant reminder of who God is.

One of the greatest traditions you could begin in your family would be to record spiritual landmarks in your lives. When God does something for you, write it down so that you can always remind yourselves of God's goodness.

Many years ago, Barbara and I took a trip to a conference, and we needed to raise about $1,300 for our ministry.

We visited many people who invested financially in our work, and a number wrote us checks. When we arrived at the conference, we counted up the checks—they totaled $1,378.

This is a story we told our children to let them know that God provides; He meets our needs. As they have their own children, they may tell this story to them—and we hope add some similar ones of their own.

God has been faithful to you in the past. Is there any reason to think He will not provide for you today?

Discuss: Begin to record the spiritual landmarks in your family by starting a diary, journal or scrapbook.

Pray: Do you have needs right now? Remember how God has worked in your life, and express your trust in Him to meet your needs once again.

GOD HAS BEEN FAITHFUL
TO YOU IN THE PAST.
IS THERE ANY REASON TO
THINK HE WILL NOT PROVIDE
FOR YOU TODAY?

THE SEVENTY-TIMES-SEVEN CLUB

Then Peter came and said to Him, "Lord, how often shall my brother sin against me and I forgive him? Up to seven times?" Jesus said to him, "I do not say to you, up to seven times, but up to seventy times seven."

MATTHEW 18:21-22

With these words, Jesus Christ formed one of the most exclusive clubs in the world—the Seventy-Times-Seven Club. He wants you to forgive each other an infinite number of times, not just when you feel like it. By an act of your will, you must put away resentment and the desire to punish the person who has wronged you.

Families can't function without forgiveness. Living together in close quarters means we inevitably have our toes stepped on. But forgiveness is hard for some people, partly because of several misconceptions about what it involves.

Here are some things forgiveness isn't:

1. *Forgiveness isn't excusing or condoning sin.* It doesn't involve changing your attitude about right and wrong.

2. *Forgiveness isn't forgetting a person's sin.* God has that power, but we do not. Forgiveness means that even though you remember the hurt, you give up the need to punish the other person.

3. *Forgiveness isn't denying your pain, hurt or anger.* It may take time for your feelings to catch up and begin to fall in line with your decision to forgive.

4. *Forgiveness isn't stuffing your grief.* There is genuine pain due to hurt. It may take time for the wound to heal, even though you forgive the person who offended you.

5. *Forgiveness isn't necessarily instant and full reconciliation.* Even when you forgive, it can take time and effort by both parties to rebuild trust.

Now that we've discussed what forgiveness is *not*, in the next devotional we'll look at what it *is*.

Discuss: Which of these misconceptions about forgiveness have you or your mate believed? How have they hurt your relationship?

Pray: Pray that a spirit of forgiveness will be stronger in your marriage relationship than the desire to nurse hurt feelings and punish each other.

FORGIVENESS MEANS
THAT EVEN THOUGH YOU
REMEMBER THE HURT, YOU
GIVE UP THE NEED TO PUNISH
THE OTHER PERSON.

LOOKING AT GOD'S EXAMPLE

Be kind to one another, tender-hearted, forgiving each other, just as God in Christ also has forgiven you.

EPHESIANS 4:32

John Wesley, founder of Methodism, was talking with General James Oglethorpe when the general remarked, "I never forgive." Wesley replied, "Then I hope, sir, that you never sin." In other words, if you can't forgive others, why should you expect God to forgive you?

Paul instructs us to forgive others "just as God in Christ also has forgiven you." This raises an interesting question: What did God in Christ do to forgive you?

To answer this question I would like to take you to a pivotal moment in human history: the crucifixion of Jesus Christ as described in Luke 23. It's a story that is rich in significance.

After Christ was betrayed, tried and unfairly convicted, after He was humiliated and scourged and jeered and spit upon, He finally suffered the cruelest indignity. The only perfect man who ever lived was hung on a cross with two criminals.

Below Him, soldiers mocked Him and stripped Him of His clothing. People sneered, "He saved others; let Him save Himself if this is the Christ of God, His Chosen One" (v. 35).

Yet Christ's response was incredible. Even at that moment, while suffering the most terrible abuse, He said, "Father, forgive them; for they do not know what they are doing" (v. 34).

This passage holds three lessons for us:

1. *Forgiveness embraces the offenders.* Christ offered forgiveness to the very people who hurt Him the most. And that's not all—He offered it to them while they were still hurting Him.
2. *Forgiveness initiates.* God desired your fellowship so much that He took the initiative in forgiving you. He did not wait for you to earn it.
3. *Forgiveness gives up all rights to punish.* God canceled your debt against Him. You deserve to die as the penalty for your sins. But God, knowing it was absolutely impossible for you to pay that debt, had Christ pay the penalty for you.

If you ever have trouble forgiving your mate, just remember what Christ did for you. And remember that you didn't deserve it.

Discuss: Recall how Christ has shown forgiveness to you. For what offenses do you find it hard to forgive your mate?

Pray: Ask God to enable you, through the Holy Spirit (who lives in you), to embrace your offenders, initiate love for them and give up all rights to punish.

Rx: Laughter

*A joyful heart is good medicine, but a broken
spirit dries up the bones.*

PROVERBS 17:22

Seriously, I like to laugh. Someone has said that laughter is the sensation of feeling good all over and showing it in one place. Laughter is one of God's lubricants for life.

Spiritual giants such as Martin Luther and C. H. Spurgeon were hooked on the stuff. Luther once kidded, "If they don't allow laughter in heaven, then I don't want to go there." He went on to add, "If the earth is fit for laughter, then surely heaven is filled with it. Heaven is the birthplace of laughter." When Spurgeon's elders asked him to tone down his humor from the pulpit, he replied, "If only you knew how much I held back, you would commend me."

Some of the most fun-loving people I know are spiritual giants of our age. Bill and Vonette Bright enjoy laughing with each other and teasing one another as much as any two I know. Some people love Chuck Swindoll's laugh almost as much as his preaching! Howard Hendricks peppers his messages with hilarious stories. It doesn't take much to imagine that our Savior, Jesus Christ, had the most winsome smile and the heartiest laugh ever.

But the way some Christians live, you'd think God had neglected to create a giggle box. They act as though enjoying a couple of laughs a week is really excessive.

We shouldn't take things so seriously that we think everything depends on us. We shouldn't be too busy to have fun. We shouldn't become so goal-oriented that we are unable to enjoy our family and laugh with them.

When was the last time you got down on all fours and "ate" your infant's tummy? Or wrestled with your adolescent? Or did something really rowdy or goofy at the dinner table? One evening we threw marshmallows at one another and laughed so hard we cried.

Laughter doesn't level life's obstacles, but it does make the climb easier to bear.

Discuss: Is the overall tone of your home one of laughter? Or of complaints and criticism? What can you do to administer the prescription of laughter?

Pray: Pray that this year God will enable you to have too much fun with your spouse and family rather than too little fun.

When was the last time you got down on all fours and "ate" your infant's tummy?

SOWING WORDS
OF PRAISE

A soothing tongue is a tree of life.

PROVERBS 15:4

Everyone loves to be praised, and your mate is no exception. William James wrote: "The deepest principle in human nature is the craving to be appreciated." And Mark Twain said, "I can live for two months on a good compliment."

Praise is valuable because it is a virtue seldom practiced! We seldom praise our employees, we seldom praise our kids, and we seldom praise our mates; yet our homes ought to be a haven where praise is liberally applied.

Carefully read these definitions of "praise": to give value, to lift up, to extol, to magnify, to honor, to commend, to applaud. If you give some creative thought to these definitions, you can come up with hundreds of ways to praise your mate. The more you verbally express your appreciation (praise), the more secure your mate will become in his or her self-esteem.

Have you ever asked someone to repeat a compliment? I have. "Oh, you really liked our FamilyLife Marriage Conference? Tell me what meant the most to you." Inwardly, I am thinking, *Yes, I need to hear this! Would you tell me one more time, so I can relish your comments for a few seconds longer?* Life can seem intolerably heavy at times, and a good, encouraging word can help to lighten the load and lift your spirits.

Arnold Glascow said, "Praise does wonders for our sense of hearing." It also does wonders for our sense of sight. When you praise your mate, you take your eyes off yourself and focus on someone else for a few brief moments. This positive focus on your mate helps to put not only his or her life in perspective but yours as well.

Discuss: When was the last time you made an effort to praise your mate? Praise your mate three times before you go to sleep tonight.

Pray: Pray that God would give you creative ideas on how to praise your mate. And if you haven't ever done so, take a few minutes in prayer to praise God for who He is and what He has done in your lives.

LIFE CAN SEEM INTOLERABLY
HEAVY AT TIMES, AND A GOOD,
ENCOURAGING WORD CAN HELP
TO LIGHTEN THE LOAD AND
LIFT YOUR SPIRITS.

A LITTLE BIT OF GRACE

BY BARBARA RAINEY

As a ring of gold in a swine's snout, so is a beautiful woman who lacks discretion.

PROVERBS 11:22

I think we wives need to give our husbands some grace—grace not to know how a woman feels or functions. I used to think, *Why doesn't Dennis just understand what I'm going through? Why doesn't he do things the way I want them done?* But I had to learn that he doesn't automatically know where I am emotionally or what I expect in different situations—unless I tell him. And if I come across as judgmental, he'll get defensive. I need to bestow some grace.

I laugh thinking about one morning when I needed to leave about the same time the kids had to be out the door. I said to Dennis, "I really need your help this morning. Could you make breakfast for everybody?"

I was thinking he would do it the way I do—prepare the meal, call the girls in and say "Here's your plate. Do you want juice?" I was really involved in serving them breakfast and talking to them.

Well, Dennis fixed them toast while watching the morning news on television. He fixed about 10 slices, stacked them on a plate and laid them on the table. When the kids got in the car, they hadn't eaten. I said, "Why didn't you eat?" They said, "Where was the food?" Dennis assumed that since the food was out, they would find it.

As I walked back into the house, I realized that Dennis's burden wasn't the same as mine. I was involved with the kids on an emotional level during breakfast, while he just wanted to complete the task while gearing up for a day at the office. He did what I asked. He just didn't do it the way I would have done it.

I decided that I needed to give him some grace.

Discuss: How well have you been communicating your feelings to your mate lately? Are you bestowing grace?

Pray: Ask the Lord to help you understand that your spouse may do things differently from you and to help you give grace instead of condemnation.

GIVE YOUR HUSBAND
SOME GRACE.

THE LIFELINE OF CONNECTION

You shall rise up before the grayheaded, and honor the aged,
and you shall revere your God; I am the LORD.

LEVITICUS 19:32

Jack Turpin of Dallas, Texas, is a busy man—but not too busy for his grandchildren. Several times a year he picks up some of his grandchildren who live in the Dallas area for what he calls Grandpa Day. Starting at 7:00 A.M., they go to a traditional spot for breakfast and then to his office. There he has a closet filled with games and books that the grandkids enjoy. After the trip to the office, they go to the sanctuary of their church and sit. Then they have lunch and return home.

A number of years ago, when one of his daughters became ill, Jack had Grandpa Camp for four days. Jack is purposely involved in his grandchildren's lives.

Let me ask you: Why are so many old people bored? Why are many of the elderly underchallenged? What keeps them going as they approach the end of life? Why do so many waste so much time chasing little white balls around a golf course?

I believe one key reason is that many grandparents are not like Jack Turpin. They are isolated from their families and are not involved in passing on a legacy.

Something tells me that in many cases the problem may be their relationships with their adult children. If you were to say to me, "I wish my parents would start making time to be grandparents," I would ask, "How much time are you spending with your parents? Are you pursuing a relationship with them?" Perhaps if we value the older generation by honoring our parents, they will value the younger generation by getting involved in their grandchildren's lives.

Do your parents feel close to you? Do they feel loved, appreciated and needed? And if they feel needed, is it for something other than just baby-sitting? If they do feel needed, then they probably already make the effort to be involved. If they don't, you can begin to restore your connection to them now.

God gives grandparents a special role in the lives of children. Children may learn some character qualities more from their grandparents than from their parents. That's the type of vision I'd like to give grandparents—helping to build another generation.

Discuss: How involved are your parents with your children? What steps can you take to help strengthen that connection?

Pray: Pray that your children will experience a great relationship with their grandparents.

COMMUNICATION OR ISOLATION?

I have had for many years a longing to come to you whenever I go to Spain—for I hope to see you in passing.

ROMANS 15:23-24

Capt. Red McDaniel rapped on his cell walls in the Hanoi Hilton—tap-tap . . . tap-tap-tap—practicing the special code that prisoners used to communicate with each other. He was risking his life, since one of the strictest rules in the celebrated Vietnamese POW camp was *No communication with other prisoners.*

His communist captors wanted to keep all "guests" isolated and vulnerable. And McDaniel had already been through that; now he was in solitary confinement. As the long hours and days passed, he met the real enemy—isolation. Without human contact or conversation, he knew only the dulling, silent darkness of loneliness.

The highlight of each day was being taken to the washroom, where he managed to whisper briefly with two other Americans. They taught him the camp code, which involved a certain number of taps or other signals that spelled out letters of the alphabet.

McDaniel, who tells of his long years of imprisonment in his book *Scars and Stripes*, saw nearly 50 of America's finest trained men go into isolation, never to be heard from again. For himself, it was either communicate or die. Prisoners who did not learn the code within 30 days of arrival would gradually start to draw inward and deteriorate. They would stop eating and slowly lose the will to live. Eventually, isolation would suck their very lives from them.

Isolation and the failure to communicate also drain life from relationships. Like the apostle Paul, most people long for intimacy and fellowship; but without communication, these essentials are impossible.

Communicate—your marriage depends on it!

Discuss: Can you recall a time when the lack of communication in your own family created a problem? How could family members work together to improve communication?

Pray: Pray that the lines of communication will stay open so that your relationship with God and your family will flourish.

COMMUNICATE—
YOUR MARRIAGE
DEPENDS ON IT!

THE NUMBER ONE THREAT TO FAMILIES

I will set no worthless thing before my eyes; I hate the work of those who fall away; it shall not fasten its grip on me.

PSALM 101:3

We once retained a research firm to ask our FamilyLife Conference guests what societal problem posed the greatest threat to their families. Was it alcohol and drug addiction? Materialism? Pornography? The breakup of families?

Nearly 36 percent answered *television*.

I shouldn't have been surprised. After all, surveys show that the average American adult watches TV a whopping 34 hours 21 minutes per week. And preschoolers are watching this plug-in drug an average of 24 hours 32 minutes per week. I guess that's what we should expect from a society that boasts almost as many homes with TVs (98 percent) as homes with indoor toilets (99.8 percent).[1]

I believe that Christian families rightly consider TV to be a threat to the family for three primary reasons.

1. *TV replaces real relationships*. Communication ceases when the TV is turned on. Who can compete

with such a vast menu of images, million-dollar commercials and programs that parade slinky, sexy bodies in front of us? I agree with the great "theologian" Erma Bombeck—she said that if a woman has a husband who watches three consecutive TV football games on a given Saturday, she should have him declared legally dead and have his estate probated!

2. *TV often undermines the commitments and moral integrity that bind a family together. Leave It to Beaver* has been replaced with sitcoms that glorify adultery, premarital sex and perverted behavior.

3. *TV robs families of time—both in quality and quantity.* After attending a FamilyLife Marriage Conference, one dad went home, unplugged the TV and lugged it to the garage. In place of the TV he hung a picture of the family. Their five-year-old son sat down on the floor and stared at the portrait; then he looked up at his dad and asked, "Does this mean we're going to become a family now?"

Discuss: How many hours of TV (or movies on video) do you think you watch each week? Your spouse? Your children? Keep track of your viewing habits for seven days; then evaluate television's grip on you and your most important relationships.

Pray: Ask God for discernment. Then make some choices that reflect your Christian beliefs.

Note

1. Nielsen Media Research, e-mail to editor, March 19, 2003; U. S. Census Bureau, "American Housing Survey for the United States: 2001," November 1, 2002. http://www.census.gov/hhes/www/housing/ahs/ahs01/tab24.html (accessed March 12, 2003).

TELEVISION IS THE
NUMBER ONE
THREAT TO FAMILIES.

THE END OF EVERY MAN

*It is better to go to a house of mourning than
to go to a house of feasting, because that is the end of
every man, and the living takes it to heart.*

ECCLESIASTES 7:2

As this verse in Ecclesiastes reminds us, knowing that we will die someday should affect how we live today.

Unfortunately, many people never seem to understand what's important in life until they are faced with the end of it. A few years ago I received a letter illustrating this truth:

Frank was a wonderful man, but he was also stern and stoic; he taught his three boys to be strong, tough, no more tears, no more hugs and only manly handshakes at bedtimes. He liked things done his way. He was not a good listener.

Frank [developed] an incurable form of cancer that spread from his legs to his lungs, spleen and various parts of his body. He was 43 years old. Within days of learning he had cancer, he gave his life to Jesus. Frank began to trust in Jesus Christ and go to Him for strength and courage.

Hugging and loving his sons became a daily absolute in their lives. He shared from his heart with the boys, cried with them, told them how proud he was of them and how very much he loved them. He became the listening, loving husband every wife dreams of.

His last four months here on earth were filled with laughter and good times with his family. Even though the cancer was taking over his body, God gave him a quality life to the end. Frank prepared his family for his death and for the task ahead of them, so that they, too, would one day reach the goal and stand before the Throne.

Frank was fortunate to learn his true priorities while he still had a chance. I can't help but think of the late Sen. Paul Tsongas, who said after his third bout with cancer, "I think of all the fathers who have young children and play golf all day Saturday and Sunday. They've never had cancer. I think of the husbands who never voice their affections for their wives. They've never had cancer."[1]

Discuss: What would you do if you learned you had only one year left to live? What would your priorities be?

Pray: Ask God to give you the ability to live by those priorities.

Note

1. Paul Tsongas, "Happy to Be Here," *People* (May 3, 1993), p. 179.

IF YOU HAD ONLY
ONE YEAR LEFT TO LIVE,
WHAT WOULD YOUR
PRIORITIES BE?

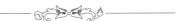

PLEASING YOUR MATE

BY BARBARA RAINEY

So teach us to number our days.

PSALM 90:12

One of the greatest sacrifices you can make to please your mate is to give your time. You can make more money and you can buy more flowers, but you can't make or buy more time. Each day is made up of 24 hours—nothing will change that.

We're all short of time. Psalm 90:12 admonishes us to "number our days." How many days do you have left? How will you use them?

I have always had an interest in art, and I enjoy looking at paintings in art galleries and museums. When we married, Dennis thought art museums were great places in which to get bored quickly. But to please me, he has spent time with me visiting quite a few museums.

In contrast, although Dennis has always loved fishing, I had no appreciation for the sport when we married. I tended to agree with the person who said, "A fisherman is a jerk on one end of a line waiting for a jerk on the other end." But to please Dennis, I did a lot of fishing during the early years of our marriage. Later, when our growing population of children made it impossible for me to go fishing with him, I encouraged him to go alone or with other men, and later, when our children were old enough, to take them along.

In the process of pleasing one another, we have become richer. Our horizons have expanded. I have learned that there is skill, patience, perseverance and reward in fishing. I no longer consider it a waste of time. Fishing has become important to me because it's part of what makes Dennis who he is. We have great vacation memories of fishing at night while our children were asleep.

To give of your time requires the greatest sacrifice. Take time for a quiet walk or a scenic drive. Above all else, simply take time for each other. If blood is the gift of life, then time is the gift of love.

Discuss: What arrangements can you make to spend more time with your mate during the next week? Each of you share one thing that you like to do together.

Pray: Pray that you will build your marriage around Jesus Christ and that you will develop some common interests that both of you can enjoy.

LIVING WITH DIFFERENCES

BY BARBARA RAINEY

Make my joy complete by being of the same mind, maintaining the same love, united in spirit, intent on one purpose.

PHILIPPIANS 2:2

*I*t's one thing to acknowledge that differences make you strong as a couple, but it's another to figure out how to live with those differences! I have a few suggestions for you.

Pray for yourself. Ask God to examine your attitudes and motives and to give you a greater capacity to understand, accept and even appreciate your mate's differences.

When we were first married, Dennis's free spirit and impulsiveness tended to drive my disciplined nature crazy. I felt that we had no schedule, no budget and no regular devotions. I remember praying diligently for God to change all the things in Dennis I didn't like. Then I realized my attitude needed to be changed. In time I began to see how much I needed his spontaneity to balance my tendency to be rigid and controlling.

Talk about differences with your mate. Tell him you are not rejecting him and that you remain committed. If you find that your mate is not emotionally prepared to discuss a touchy issue, leave the subject alone.

If your mate is willing to talk about a difference that is bothering you, *share your feelings without accusing him and pointing the finger of blame.* Let him know you realize you're not perfect and that you understand him, or want to understand him, in this area.

If your mate considers a difference to be a weakness, *ask if you can help.* Then, at the end of your discussion, remind your mate again of your commitment and acceptance. We call this the bookend principle. Just as bookends are used to prop up books that contain truth, so your reminders of love and complete acceptance at both ends of the discussion will support the truth of what you've said. And it makes the truth a whole lot *easier* to hear!

Discuss: How do your and your spouse's differences make you stronger as a couple?

Pray: Ask God for the ability to discuss differences openly, without being defensive or feeling threatened.

DUSTING EACH OTHER OFF

Death and life are in the power of the tongue,
and those who love it will eat its fruit.

PROVERBS 18:21

*P*icture yourself awaiting your turn to bat while the major league baseball pitcher takes his warm-up pitches. The pitcher's first pitch to the first batter sails over the catcher's head and slams into the screen. The next one burrows wildly in the dirt and bounces up, almost hitting you in the on-deck circle—20 feet from home plate!

Nervous and uncertain, you finally step up to the plate. After three swings at the missile burning across the plate at 90 miles an hour, you're glad to trot back to the safety of the dugout.

Ryne Duren, former pitcher for the New York Yankees, liked to intimidate batters like that. He was known as the patron saint of the psych-out. He knew how to mentally harass opposing batters, "dusting them off" with an assortment of wildly launched pitches that left them terrified.

Unfortunately, words are sometimes hurled like that in the home. Instead of hurling a baseball, we launch hurtful, intimidating words at each other, inflicting fear, pain and guilt. We learn what the wise man meant when he said death is in "the power of the tongue."

Winston Churchill was a master at dusting off his opponents with such missiles. Once, after he had overindulged, his spiteful opponent Lady Astor said to him, "Mr. Prime Minister, I perceive you are drunk." Churchill smiled and replied, "Yes, Lady Astor, and you are ugly. But tomorrow I shall be sober."

Even though you may be just as skillful with the quick retort, what do you gain when you fire off such verbal volleys? Scripture warns that those who love to use "the power of the tongue" destructively will eat its fruits. Often, those fruits are resentment, discord and revenge. Destructive words not only hurt others, but they also poison our relationships.

Discuss: What is the overall tone of conversation in your family? What influence do you as parents have on this issue? What can you do to lessen the inclination to attack each other with hurtful words?

Pray: Since Jesus Christ is the Word, pray that your word in every aspect of home life will reflect His identity as Prince of Peace and Mediator.

DEATH AND LIFE
ARE IN THE POWER OF
THE TONGUE.

PROVERBS 18:21

GROWING UP

When I was a child, I used to speak as a child,
think as a child, reason as a child; when I became a man,
I did away with childish things.

1 CORINTHIANS 13:11

The apostle Paul knew that kids will be kids and that as children, we behave childishly. But he also pointed out that as we grow up, we must set aside childish behavior and become more mature.

Children are by nature petty, hurtful and faultfinding in their relationships. They speak rashly, rudely and selfishly, with little concern for how their words will affect their parents and others.

Children think life revolves around them. They're self-righteous. They think they're always right and that others are at fault, even when the evidence declares them guilty. I'll never forget the time one of our daughters came to the table with chocolate on her face—clear evidence that she'd been into the cookie jar. Evidence or not, she insisted she was not guilty! Parents often face such tests in teaching their kids to tell the truth, to be straightforward and honest.

We tell our kids, "It's time to grow up!"

And of course some of the unhappiest husband-wife relationships are those in which one or both haven't really grown up. They are still petty, hurtful and faultfinding. They still speak rashly and rudely, with little regard for how their words may hurt each other. They still think life revolves around them and have trouble taking responsibility for their actions and choices and admitting when they are wrong. They blame, ridicule and find ways to get back at their spouses.

They speak, think and reason as children.

It dawned on me one day, in the middle of an argument with Barbara, that it was time I grew up, that I stopped acting like the kids. And you know what? I realized if I was going to be a man, I couldn't act like a child. And so, just like Paul, I put away childish things.

Discuss: Think of some tense times you've had with your mate recently. Can you detect in your own attitude any childishness? What steps can you take to help your own children mature?

Pray: Pray, "Lord God, help me be a man and put away childish words, attitudes and actions. May Your Holy Spirit empower me this day. Amen."

IT'S TIME FOR US
TO GROW UP.

"ME FIRST!"— CROWDING IN

Be devoted to one another in brotherly love;
give preference to one another in honor.

ROMANS 12:10

$f$ew of us born before 1958 will forget those long gasoline lines that occurred during the oil crisis in 1973 and 1974. Naturally, some greedy people wanted to cut in line to get ahead of others. Newspapers carried stories about everything from profanity and lawsuits to stabbings and shootings, as people fought for their places in line to get gas.

One woman cut in front of a motorbike. The cyclist slowly got off his bike, took off his helmet and glasses and proceeded to let the air out of all four of her tires, while she sat helplessly, caught in the line!

But the most creative stunt I read about was the young man who got cut off and retaliated by unscrewing the gas cap from the offending car, replacing it with his own locking gas cap and driving off—with the gas-cap key in his pocket!

All too often we get caught up in the rush to the shallow well of "me-first-ism." "We're number one!" becomes not just a cheer at a football game but a personal motto. But selfishness is possibly the most dangerous threat to oneness that any marriage can face.

The apostle Paul's counsel, therefore, becomes a prescription for marital oneness: "Give preference to one another in honor." Marriage provides the opportunity to live life for someone other than yourself and to avoid the terrible mind-set: "All I've got is me. I can't depend on anyone else."

Discuss: How can you show preference to your spouse? Think of 10 ways and then do one of them!

Pray: Pray that God would give all members of your family the desire to serve one another and that they'd feel no compulsion to compete to be "first in line."

SELFISHNESS IS
POSSIBLY THE MOST
DANGEROUS THREAT TO
ONENESS THAT ANY
MARRIAGE CAN FACE.

BUILDING BLOCKS FOR A HOME

*By wisdom a house is built, and by understanding
it is established; and by knowledge the rooms are filled
with all precious and pleasant riches.*

PROVERBS 24:3-4

The wise man Solomon describes three fundamentals for building not only a house but also a home.

By wisdom a house is built. I define "wisdom" as "skill in everyday living." Solomon also said, "The fear of the LORD is the beginning of wisdom" (Prov. 9:10). When homes are built on godly wisdom, family members respond to circumstances according to God's design, not their own.

A wise home builder recognizes God as the Architect and Builder of the family. As you search the Scriptures and ask God for wisdom, He supplies the skill to build your home.

By understanding it is established. "Understanding" means "responding to life's circumstances with insight"—having a perspective that looks at life through God's eyes. When you have God's perspective of your mate and children, you accept each other's differences and learn how different personalities can complement each other.

A couple once shared with me how they finally understood this. They explained that at one time, the husband had said, "My wife is a prosecuting attorney. I feel like she prosecutes from eight to five and persecutes from five to eight." After a year and a half of trying to change her, he finally understood that he didn't have to compete with her strong personality. "I can let her be who she is and not feel insecure about who I am," he said.

By knowledge the rooms are filled. Our culture virtually worships information. But information without application is an empty deity. Every Sunday morning thousands of preachers present polished gems—outstanding biblical knowledge. But what do we, the parishioners, usually do? At 11:55 A.M. the preacher finishes, we sing a song, a prayer is prayed, and we leave at 12:00 P.M. The knowledge Solomon speaks of is more than information. It is knowledge that results in conviction *and* application.

Discuss: Which of these three building blocks is most evident in your home? Which needs the most work?

Pray: Pray that God will deepen your wisdom, sharpen your understanding and enrich your knowledge of what He wants you, your marriage and your family to be.

As you search
the Scriptures and
ask God for wisdom,
He supplies the skill to
build your home.

F amilyLife has been bringing couples the wonderful news of God's blueprints for marriage since 1976.

Today we are strengthening hundreds of thousands of homes each year in the United States and around the world through:

- **Weekend to Remember**™ conferences

- **I Still Do**® conferences

- **HomeBuilders Couples Series**® small-group Bible studies

- **"FamilyLife Today,"** our daily, half-hour radio program, and four other nationally syndicated broadcasts

- A comprehensive Web site, **www.familylife.com**, featuring marriage and parenting tips, daily devotions, conference information, and a wide range of resources for strengthening families

- Unique marriage and family **connecting resources**

Through these outreaches, FamilyLife is effectively developing godly families who reach the world one home at a time.

FAMILYLIFE™
Bringing Timeless Principles Home

Dennis Rainey, Executive Director
1-800-FL-TODAY (358-6329)
www.familylife.com

A division of Campus Crusade for Christ